Mysterious Thelonious

Chris Raschka

ORCHARD BOOKS   NEW YORK

Orchard Books, 95 Madison Avenue, New York, NY 10016

Manufactured in the United States of America
Printed by Barton Press, Inc.
Bound by Horowitz/Rae
The text of this book is hand lettered.
The illustrations are watercolor
reproduced in full color.

Library of Congress Cataloging-in-Publication Data
Raschka, Christopher.
Mysterious Thelonious / Chris Raschka.   p.   cm.
Summary: Matches the tones of the chromatic scale
to the values of the color wheel in presenting a
portrait of the work of the Afro-American jazz
musician and composer of "Misterioso."
ISBN 0-531-30057-9   ISBN 0-531-33057-5 (lib. bdg.)
1. Monk, Thelonious—Pictorial works—Juvenile
literature.   [1. Monk, Thelonious.   2. Musicians.
3. Jazz.   4. Afro-Americans—Biography.]   I. Title.
ML3930.M66R37   1997
786.2'165'092—dc21   97-6994

10 9 8 7 6 5 4 3 2 1

for Dick Jackson

his sic. and mu-

no

no

had

a-

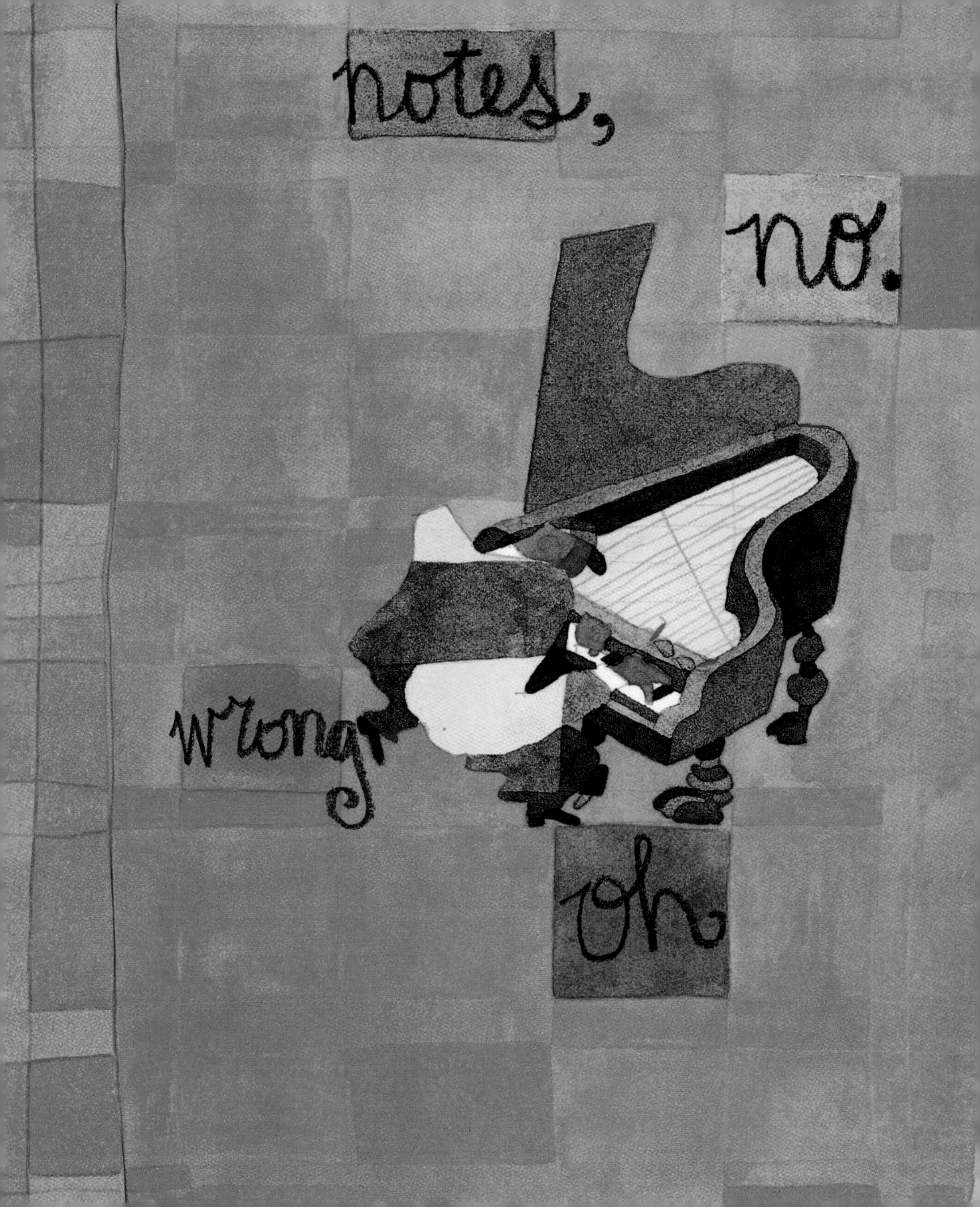
notes,
no.
wrong
oh

stor-

is

a

This

sic

ly

mu-

love-

one

played

not

He

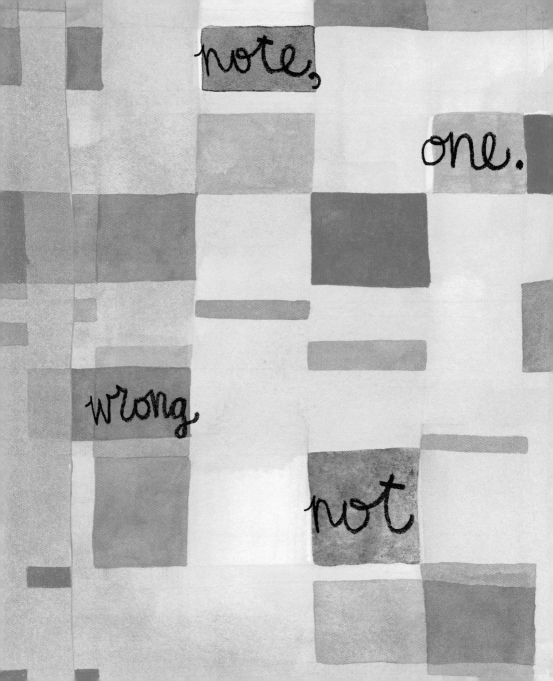

no

pi-

a-

His

none, one.

had not

mu-

played

the

He

mu-

is

the

Jazz

This is a pic-

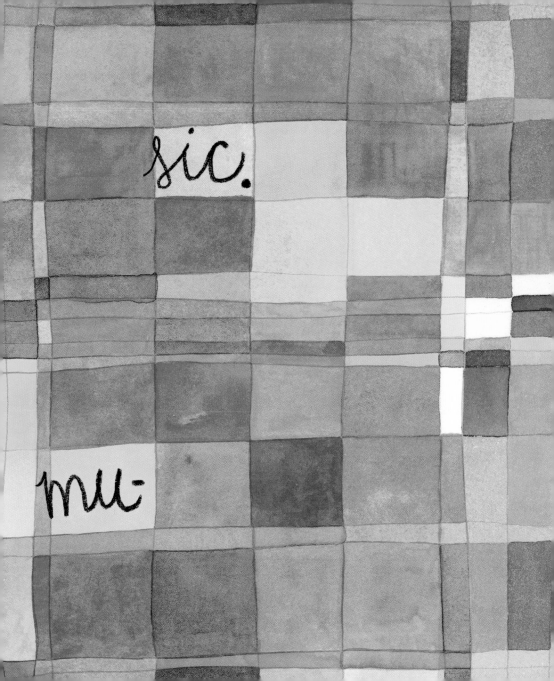

ous

ter-   lo-

so

i-

mys-   The-

Oh

ous

ter-   lo-

ous,

i-

mys-   The-

ni-

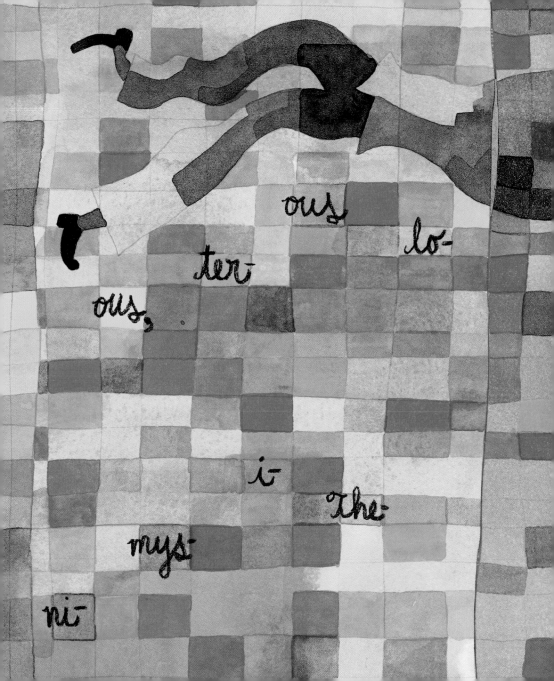

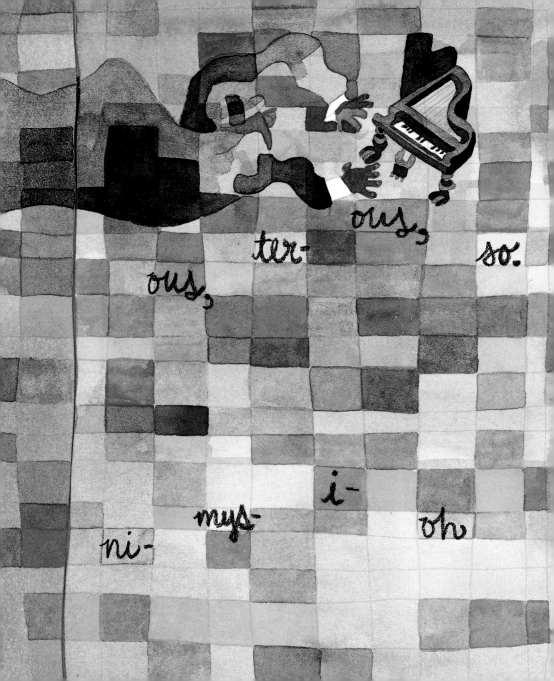

Date Due

PRINTED IN U.S.A. CAT. NO. 23231